Aerial view of the Margerie Glacier.

THE LEADING EDGE

Look at a map of Southeast Alaska. The mountains, islands, inlets and straits tend to run in long, north-south patterns, each parallel to the next. Like the leading edge of a carpet that rumples when pushed from behind, Southeast Alaska has rumpled for millions of years as our continent has drifted west by northwest over the floor of the Pacific crustal plate. Rocks from the Pacific floor have piled into those on the edge of North America, creating the coastal mountains we see today. Nearly every major rock type—igneous, sedimentary and metamorphic—is represented here. And nearly all of them are smashed, folded and faulted into, over and under each other. To decipher an exact chronology of the bedrock geology here is to invite a headache. One geologist calls it "the chaotic coast."

What shaped the land, however, was another architect of immense proportion and power: the Ice Age. The tectonics of continental drift fractured the land into long, longitudinal breaks, called faults, and it was these weak spots—the paths of least resistance—that the glaciers followed, digging the deep U-shaped troughs that later filled with seawater as the glaciers retreated. Notice Chatham Strait, Lynn Canal, Gastineau Channel, Stephens Passage, Clarence Strait and every other stitch of Southeast Alaska's waterways. Seawater fills them today, but it was ice that created them.

Fireweed and backdrop of the Fairweather Mountains, Glacier Bay.

ALASKA'S INSIDE PASSAGE

BY KIM HEACOX

ALBION
PUBLISHING GROUP

Sitka black-tailed deer.

Shooting stars, Indian paintbrush and buttercups, Baranof Island.

ACKNOWLEDGMENTS

Our special thanks to Neil Hagadorn and Carl Holguin, Tongass National Forest; Bruce Paige, Glacier Bay National Park; Gary Candelaria and Tim Stone, Sitka National Historic Park; and Gary Lidholm, USDA Forest Service.

PHOTO CREDITS

Tom Bean: Front cover; inside front cover; 4 top; 6-7; 8; 9; 10 inset; 12 left; 16; 18; 19; 21; 26; 27 bottom; 28; 31 bottom; 32 left; 34; 35; 37; 38; 39; 46; 47 top; inside back cover; back flap. *Gary Braasch:* 23; 47 bottom. *Randy Brandon:* 33 inset. *Maxine Cass:* Front flap; 5; 13; 14; 27 inset. *John Evarts:* 17. *Francois Gohier:* 29 top and bottom; 30 top and bottom. *Kim Heacox:* 4 bottom; 10-11; 15; 31 top; 32 right; 40 top; 44; 45; back cover. *Fred Hirschmann:* 2-3; 20; 27 top; 36. *Jeff Schultz:* 42 left. *Linda Trujillo:* Inside front cover. *USDA Forest Service:* 22; 24 top and bottom; 25; 41. *Harry Walker:* 12 right; 22 bottom; 33 top; 40 bottom; 42 right; 43.

ALBION
PUBLISHING GROUP

Albion Publishing Group
Lorie Bacon, Publisher
924 Anacapa Street, Suite 3A
Santa Barbara, CA 93101
(805) 963-6004

Written by Kim Heacox and Darcy Ellington
Edited by Janie Freeburg and John Evarts
Designed by Gay Hagen
Reprint coordinated by Angela Tripp
Reprint design and production
by Joanne Station

Second Edition 1993

Printed in Hong Kong
through AsiaPrint, Ltd. USA
ISBN: 1-880352-30-3

Right: A colony of kittiwakes.
Preceding page: Mt. Edgecumbe rises above the fog blanketing Sitka Sound.

Sunrise on Mt. Fairweather.

C O N T E N T S

CHAPTER ONE

THE PASSAGE'S PAST

Ice Will Suffice

Left: Aerial view of a glacier.
Above: The remarkable ice worm.

There was no Inside Passage 15,000 years ago. A solid sea of ice buried the land, and the mountain peaks we see today were merely islands in an ocean of glaciers. This was the twilight of the Ice Age; the last hurrah of the climatic pendulum that had sent great tides of continental glaciers flowing and ebbing over North America many times in the last two million years. When the massive glaciers retreated they opened up a new geography of handsome shores and waterways. Long fingers of the Pacific Ocean flowed into the inlets, and blankets of vegetation healed the hillsides. The glaciers are still here—there are nearly 70 of them in Southeast Alaska—but they're a small fraction of the size they once were.

A flight over the Juneau, Stikine or Brady Icefields reveals to the mind's eye how all of Southeast Alaska looked 15,000 years ago. Two hundred inches of snow can fall in these icefields each year. Glaciers flow from them like rivers from lakes—a dozen from Glacier Bay's Brady Icefield; a dozen from the Stikine Icefield, between Wrangell and Petersburg; and 30 from the Juneau Icefield, to the east and north of its namesake city.

They move with tremendous power, flexing over diverse terrain underneath while breaking into crevasses on their brittle surfaces. It's not the ice itself that erodes the mountains, but rocks embedded in the ice. Sediment tumbles down the mountainsides onto the margins of the glaciers and squeezes into the middle like a dark highway centerline, forming a moraine when two glaciers merge into one.

Spores, pollen and dust blow onto the surface of the glaciers, and a species of algae grows there as well. Perhaps the most remarkable glacial lifeform of all is the ice worm, a dark, inch-long relative of the earthworm. It manages to live on the surfaces of the glaciers, probably by eating the algae, spores and pollen.

Glaciers have budgets balanced between income and expenditures. Income is the rate of snow accumulation at higher elevations while expenditure is the rate of melting at lower elevations. At equilibrium—when neither exceeds the other—a glacial terminus remains stationary. Should snowfall increase over many years, thereby creating more ice, the glacial terminus would likely advance. Conversely, glaciers often retreat following a period of snowfall decrease. This doesn't mean glaciers flow backward nor upslope; they always flow forward and downslope. Only the terminus of a glacier advances or retreats.

Over the past several thousand years the ice budget apparently has been tipped with snow losses exceeding gains. Most of the glaciers of Southeast Alaska, progeny of the local climate, have been starved of new ice. Underfed and overextended, they retreat. Some glaciers which gather snow from higher elevations are an exception to the glacial budget trend. As if in rebellion, glaciers such as the Hubbard and the Taku in the Tongass National Forest are still advancing.

Glacial ice isn't the same stuff that forms in your refrigerator. It's more dense and less porous, and may develop crystals half a meter in diameter. In some respects it's a metamorphic rock, having hardened and crystallized under tremendous pressures over long periods of time. When hit by visible light the ice absorbs the red end of the spectrum and reflects back the blues. The color is especially intense on overcast days.

Many of the glaciers in Southeast Alaska are tidewater glaciers, ending not on land, but in the sea where their steep, vertical faces calve massive icebergs into the water. The bergs drift down the inlets and melt into the sea, or become stranded on shore by the tides. On the average, only about 15 percent of an iceberg floats above water. But some carry heavy loads of rock and sediment, and float just below the surface, giving boaters nightmares.

Icebergs can split apart without warning. Even in sunshine they melt faster below the waterline than above; they grow lopsided and roll over. Boaters with more courage than common sense have climbed aboard icebergs in the inlets of Southeast Alaska. They've set up tents on the bergs. One couple climbed out of their kayak to dine on an iceberg, and as they began to sip their wine the berg rolled over and tossed them unceremoniously into the sea.

The Le Conte Glacier flows down to the sea. Inset: Blue icebergs in Muir Inlet, Glacier Bay National Park.

The People of Eagle and Raven

The Tlingit and Haida Indians of Southeast Alaska did more than survive, they excelled. They are living proof that rich cultures arise from a rich environment.

The climate was mild, food was bountiful and

Carved faces, Totem Bight State Park.

A group of totems near Ketchikan.

opportunities for social pastimes—travel, trade, art and religion—were abundant. Their canoes were 70 feet long and held 50 or 60 paddlers. They would travel 1,500 miles down to Puget Sound and back, trading along the way. They could fashion halibut hooks, track game and read the seas with an expertise that dumbfounded the early white settlers.

Upon hearing that the Haida were excellent mariners, a Yankee steamboat captain challenged them to a race across a broad stretch of open water. The Haidas agreed and watched as the captain departed full steam ahead. Suddenly the seas shifted and the Haidas pushed off in their canoe. They paddled onto a large seaswell, surfed past the steamer, and were standing on the opposite shore when it arrived.

Tlingit and Haida mythology teaches an abiding respect for nature. A rock or tree is as alive to them as a whale or a bear. They believe everything has a spirit. A slain bear is welcomed home with a speech and placed in a seat of honor for a day.

Life is a continuum to these native people. They don't take fish and animals, they borrow them. The idea of owning land is incomprehensible. They belong to the land, not vice versa; it's as simple as that. Two men arguing over the ownership of land would seem as absurd to them as two fleas arguing over ownership of the dog they live on.

Family lineage is the principal theme in their totems, blankets, baskets and ceremonies. Every design tells a story and preserves a heritage passed down through countless generations. Crowning the designs are Eagle and Raven, the two great social divisions, or moieties, to which everyone belongs. The divisions are matrilineal. Children adopt the moiety of their mother but must marry into the opposite moiety, that of their father. Thus, in every family one parent is an Eagle and the other is a Raven. These two great branches further divide like the limbs of a tree into kinship clans and thence into house groups.

An estimated 10,000 Haida and Tlingit lived along the coasts of British Columbia and Southeast Alaska when white men first arrived 200 years ago. The Haida lived to the south; the Tlingit to the north. One explorer after another penned

Fur and beads adorn a Tlingit coat.

glowing accounts of a proud and prosperous people living along the Inside Passage. In 1794, Captain George Vancouver described a Tlingit chief near the present site of Sitka: "He was dressed in a much more superb style than any chief we had hitherto seen on this coast, and he supported a degree of state consequence.... His external robe was a very fine large garment that reached from his neck down to his heels, made of wool from the mountain, neatly variegated with several colours, and edged, and otherwise decorated with little tufts, or frogs of woollen yarn, dyed of various colours.... The whole exhibited a magnificent appearance, and indicated a taste for dress and ornament that we had not supposed the natives of these regions to possess."

Southeast Alaska's rich heritage is due in large part to the Tlingit and Haida cultures. Their totems, blankets, basketry and legends are the archives of this land. Their family crests are thousands of years old. A colorfully designed blanket wrapped around a Tlingit reminds him of who he is, where he came from and where he's going. It keeps him warm in spirit as well as in body.

Great White Sails

Great white sails were on the western horizon; the Inside Passage would never be the same.

The first to arrive were Vitus Bering and Alexei Chirikof sailing under the Russian coat of arms in 1741. Separated by a storm shortly after departing Kamchatka, they sailed east by different routes across a cold, featureless sea toward a land that existed more in fable than in fact.

Chirikof, commanding the *St. Paul,* glimpsed North America off Prince of Wales Island in July, then sailed north and anchored near present-day Sitka where he sent a party ashore. They failed to return, so he sent a second party after them. They, too, failed to return. Two canoes of Tlingits then paddled out to the *St. Paul,* yelled something at the Russians, and departed. With no more small boats at his disposal, Chirikof weighed anchor and sailed away, the fate of his men unknown to this day.

Vitus Bering fared even worse. He was an old, sickly man trying to live a young man's dream, and the voyage hadn't set well with him from the start. Commanding the *St. Peter,* he landed north of Southeast Alaska, on Kayak Island near the present community of Cordova. With Bering was the German naturalist Georg Wilhelm Stellar, who went ashore for ten short hours to gather plant and animal specimens never before recorded by white men, including a dark-crested jay named in his honor. Stellar was Alaska's first naturalist—and Kayak Island became "Alaska's Plymouth Rock."

Bering himself did not go ashore on Kayak Island. That fall, while attempting to sail home, he shipwrecked on the Komandorski Islands, halfway between the tip of the Aleutians and the Kamchatka Peninsula, and he died there that winter. His crew managed to build a crude boat from the wreckage of the *St. Peter* to sail back to Kamchatka in the spring. Their return was hailed as a miracle, but the czar was most excited by what they brought home with them—900 glossy, luxurious sea otter pelts that fetched premium prices from Chinese merchants. The Russians had discovered their own El Dorado; the rush for furs was on.

The Tlingits interpreted the white sails as the great thunderbird of their mythology—an omen. But their curiosity turned to contempt as the white men brandished a greed and arrogance hardly conceivable to the Tlingits. It was just the beginning.

Killing thousands of sea otters along the way, the Russians followed the Aleutian Islands. They indentured the native Aleut peoples, and arrived in Southeast Alaska with an insatiable appetite for furs and profits. Alexander Baranof, governor of the newly formed Russian-American Fur Company, founded a colonial headquarters on Kodiak Island in 1799. In 1808, the company's headquarters moved to New Archangel, known today as Sitka.

Tweny-six years later, the Russians established an outpost, which was strategically located near the mouth of the mighty Stikine River for access to the inland fur trade. They called it Redoubt Saint Dionysius; the name was later changed to Fort Stikine and then finally to Wrangell.

Above: A Tlingit house front at the Visitor's Center entrance, Sitka National Historical Park.

Right: A solitary kayaker at North Sandy Cove, Glacier Bay.

Not to be outdone, Spain, France and England sent great white sails to Southeast Alaska on the heels of the Russians. Battling scurvy and rough seas, Juan Perez journeyed up the west coast of North America as far as Prince of Wales Island in 1774, and on to Baranof Island in 1775.

Jean Francois Galaup de la Perouse, a preeminent French scientist as well as a mariner, explored Southeast Alaska in 1786. But like so many sailors of his time, tragedy befell him. Historians wonder if it was a premonition that made him stop in Kamchatka and arrange to have his journals sent overland to Paris, for they remain the only evidence of his Alaska explorations. From Kamchatka he and his two ships, the *Astrolabe* and *Boussole,* turned toward Indonesia and vanished into the southern seas.

Captain James Cook, regarded by many historians as the greatest explorer of all time, lead the HMS *Resolution* and the HMS *Discovery* up the coast of Southeast Alaska in 1778. He named Mount Edgecumbe (off Sitka) and Mount Fairweather (the highest point in Glacier Bay National Park and Preserve) before continuing into subarctic waters on his third and final epic voyage of the Pacific. Later that same year he died at the hands of natives on the shores of Hawaii.

Serving under Cook were two men destined to earn their own pages in the history books—William Bligh and George Vancouver. Even though he later became governor of Australia, Bligh's reputation, tarnished by the mutiny on the *Bounty,* was dubious at best. But Captain George Vancouver returned to Southeast Alaska in 1793 and 1794. Like his mentor, Cook, Vancouver had a penchant for meticulous mapping. He sent his longboats through the fog and ice of Icy Strait, Lynn Canal and Chatham Strait to make charts so accurate they remained in use 100 years later.

By the 1850s, the Russians had harvested sea otters to the point of near extinction, thus eliminating the very resource that had sustained their Alaskan operations. With the fur trade nearly dead, the czar decided to sell Alaska. England expressed a strong interest, but because the country had recently opposed Russia in the Crimean War, it lost out to the United States. The Stars and Stripes were raised over Sitka in 1867 when U.S. Secretary of State William Seward agreed to pay 7.2 million dollars for Alaska—or "Seward's Folly" as people called it. It would take 100 years before America realized the folly was really a fortune.

Interior of the "Trail of '98" Museum, Skagway.

Skagway's goldrush-era cemetery.

The Gold Stampedes

"Look more closely. The eye catches movement. The mountain is alive. There is a continuous moving train; they are perceptible only by their movement, just as ants are. The moving train is zigzagging across the towering face of the precipice, up, up into the sky, even at the very top. See! They are going against the sky. They are human beings, but never did men look so small."

Thus wrote Edwin Tappan Adney in *Harper's Weekly* magazine in 1897, describing one of the wildest chapters in the history of Alaska—the Klondike Gold Rush. Up the Inside Passage sailed tens of thousands of optimists enroute to Canada's Yukon Territoy, each of them thinking he'd be the one to strike it rich. They disembarked in the rowdy, lawless towns of Dyea and Skagway, and from there trudged over the Chilkoot and White Passes where Canadian mounties required each man bring at least 1,000 pounds of food and gear with him. Some made the long, icy, 45 degree ascent 20 times or more, each trip carrying up to 100 pounds of beans, bacon, picks and shovels on his back. And for all that, not one in a hundred hit the jackpot. But in the long run the most important element of the gold rush wasn't the gold, but the search itself.

It all began when a dirt poor miner named George Washington Carmack made a strike on Canada's Klondike River in 1896 and stepped off a steamer in Seattle a year later with a suitcase filled with gold. He was a millionaire. Newspaper headlines flashed around the country—"GOLD!"—and people went nuts. No amount of sanity could insulate a man from the temptation of the Klondike. The farmer dropped his plough, the banker his papers, the dentist his pliers, and the carpenter his hammer to find their fortunes in gold. Only a fool would work for wages, they said. Even the mayor of Seattle packed up and headed north.

Quiet Alaskan shores erupted into shanty towns where stampeders ambled up and down rutted streets, trying to navigate through the shoals of conmen, bunco artists and over-priced fandango

View from the top of Chilkoot Pass.

parlors. Fortunes were won and lost in a day. Men aged quickly as they bent their backs from sunup to sundown in frigid streams by winter, and in swarms of insects by summer. The work was never easy, yet the hope of wealth kept their noses to the ground.

Steamers plied the waters of the Inside Passage with increasing regularity, off-loading men with dreams while on-loading others with broken dreams. It was a wild and zany moment in history; one that inspired the prose of Jack London and the poetry of Robert Service, catapulting Southeast Alaska out of obscurity and into the imaginations of people around the world. Never again would the Inside Passage be an unheard-of place.

Skagway wasn't the only Southeast town born of gold. Nearly 20 years earlier, in 1880, Richard Harris and Joe Juneau had stumbled up a creek off Gastineau Channel and found a rich pocket of gold-bearing quartz. The town of Juneau grew like a weed as miners arrived out of thin air to invade the creeks and hillsides. Rich strikes the following years kept the town's momentum going. John Treadwell, an erstwhile carpenter who turned miner, built a 120-stamp mill in 1883 that produced 70 million dollars in gold. It was the largest operation of its kind in the world.

But the first gold strike to fuel further exploration of Alaska occurred in 1861 when a fur trader, Buck Choquette, found nuggets on the upper Stikine River. Wrangell, then a quiet trading post at the mouth of the river, suddenly boomed into a boisterous tent town of fifteen thousand. Other strikes lured men farther north to Windham Bay, Baranof Island, Juneau and finally to the Klondike. Like a chain reaction, gold fever spread up Alaska's Inside Passage and chartered a course of human settlement still on the maps today.

Two Alaskas

When railroad magnate Edward H. Harriman fell ill in late 1898, his doctors suggested that he take a peaceful cruise at sea. He could take along friends, but no railroad men. This was to be a vacation for rest and relaxation. Incapable of doing anything in a small way, Harriman filled the steamer *George W. Elder* with a "who's who" roster of America's premier scientists, naturalists, artists, writers and photographers, and set sail for Alaska in May, 1899. This became the famous Alaska Harriman Expedition—a grand and fittingly Victorian adventure in the twilight of the 19th century.

John Muir, the indefatigable naturalist and founder of the Sierra Club, signed the roster as "an author and student of glaciers" and called the Elder "a floating university." John Burroughs, the leading nature writer of his day, cowered a bit in the company of such preeminent scientists. "I keep mum lest I show my ignorance," he wrote.

Other passengers included George Bird Grinnell, anthropologist, zoologist, editor of *Forest and Stream* magazine, and founder of the National Audubon Society; C. Hart Merriam, first chief of the U.S. Biological Survey (later the U.S. Fish & Wildlife Service) and co-founder of the National Geographic Society; Henry Gannett, chief geographer of the U.S. Geological Survey; Frederick V. Colville, America's foremost botanist; William H. Dall, explorer and anthropologist (for whom the Dall sheep is named), and many illustrious others destined to shape the beginnings of a conservation ethic in America.

They sailed the Inside Passage not in search of furs or gold, but of knowledge and inspiration. They found two Alaskas—one of matchless resources to be tapped for a young, growing nation; and another of matchless beauty to be preserved forever from the bottomless basket of human greed. They asked the pivotal question still debated today: "Can Alaska be both?" Among the many fine wordsmiths who made that voyage nearly a century ago, it was Henry Gannett who penned a final piece of advice:

"There is one other asset of the Territory not yet enumerated, imponderable, and difficult to appraise, yet one of the chief assets of Alaska, if not the greatest. This is the scenery... Its grandeur is more valuable than the gold or the fish or the timber, for it will never be exhausted... If you are old, go by all means; but if you are young, wait. The scenery of Alaska is much grander than anything else of the kind in the world, and it is not well to dull one's capacity for enjoyment by seeing the finest first."

A breaching humpback whale in Kelp Bay.

Harbor seal poses on an ice floe. Right: The west arm of Glacier Bay, looking southeast.

CHAPTER TWO

A CELEBRATION OF LIFE

The Emerald Forest

Left: A totem pole peeks from the Sitka spruce forest, Sitka National Historic Park. Above: Baneberries.

This isn't just any forest. Most of Alaska's Inside Passage is within the immense Tongass National Forest, one of the greatest temperate rain forests in the world. Rain forests constitute one of the earth's most intriguing phenomena, and the Tongass is an awesome example of one of these complex and significant biological systems. It has evolved over thousands of years and is home to countless species of plant and animal life, as well as being one of the most beautiful places on the planet. The Tongass is a biome, or life zone, filled with depth, diversity and detail and wrapped like a green shawl around mountain vertebrae from ridge top to seashore. It's the kind of forest J.R.R. Tolkien or Edgar Allen Poe would invent. But there's no fiction here. This forest is real.

Stretching northward from the Canadian border to beyond Skagway, the Tongass is over 500 miles long and 100 miles wide. It encompasses some 17 million acres, over a third of which is designated wilderness land. This majestic land of forest, glaciers, mountains and waterways (there are nearly 11,000 miles of coastline) takes its name from the Tongass clan of Tlingit Indians. It was established as a national forest in 1907 by President Theodore Roosevelt and includes two national monuments—Misty Fiords and Admiralty Island.

Stepping inside the forest, sounds become muted, mosses carpet the floor and hang beardlike from giant tree limbs, and green infuses everything, even the air. The low-growing plants can be as inviting as the twin flower or dwarf dogwood, or as formidable as the thorn-covered devil's club. They can be as tasty as blueberry or salmonberry, or as deadly poisonous as the bright red baneberry.

On the average, 70 percent of the forest conifers are western hemlock. A healthy specimen can reach as high as 190 feet with a five-foot-diameter trunk. Sitka spruce, Alaska's state tree, constitute 20 percent of the forest and typically reach 160 feet in height and three feet

in diameter. The remaining conifers include western red cedar, Alaska cedar, mountain hemlock and lodgepole pine. The handsome, aromatic western red cedar grows only on the southern half of the panhandle. The Tlingit and Haida Indians preferred this wood for their totems, canoes, and houses, and cedar is still popular today for boat and roof construction.

Alders, willows, black cottonwood and mountain ash round out the inventory of trees. Some are pioneer species that grow in disturbed areas, such as land recently de-glaciated or burned by fire. Others, like willow and cottonwood, are water lovers that crowd stream and river banks.

Among the trees live many different species of wildlife. The Tongass is home to both the black and brown bear as well as the Sitka black-tailed deer. Mountain goats and numerous smaller animals are also found here, including the lynx, wolf, red fox, beaver, wolverine and weasel. Eagles roam the skies searching for fish in waters below, and marine mammals can be spotted along the coast.

To some, this land of spectacular beauty and abundance is a playground filled with exciting diversions. To others, the Tongass is an important source of jobs and wealth. To still others the mighty forest is a scenic wonder that must be preserved for future generations. It is the task of the Forest Service to balance all of the demands made on the Tongass and to manage the forest for a variety of uses. It is not always easy.

Imagine a hillside where the ground is bare and uneven. Ragged stumps protrude from the earth and the skies above are silent. A clear cut in the midst of this vast green landscape packs a visual wallop. And indeed, over the past few

Above: A floatplane provides access to remote Klacka Inlet, South Prince of Wales Wilderness.

Right: An old cabin in the hemlocks, Kupreanof Island.

years timber cutting in the forest has been highly controversial. Conservationists maintain that logging is damaging to the forest ecosystem and unprofitable to boot. On the other side, the timber companies emphasize the renewable aspects of the forest, and cite the industry's importance to both the regional and national economy. The Forest Service, which is responsible for maximizing the region's potential while protecting wildlife habitats, has been caught in the middle.

The issues were somewhat resolved by the passage of the Tongass Reform Act in 1990. The legislation set aside another million acres of land where logging is prohibited. Moreover, existing timber contracts were revised to better reflect current market conditions and reasonable harvest goals.

In addition, the Forest Service operates a second growth management program that monitors areas that have been replanted after the original trees have been removed. The goal is to develop better forest management techniques. The Forest Service is also required to work closely with native and other groups to ensure that timber cutting doesn't interfere with traditional subsistence uses of the land. Nevertheless, it will remain a challenge to find a happy medium between maximizing the use of the natural resources and preserving the fragile ecosystem.

Of course, to many visitors the Tongass seems anything but fragile. The towering mountains rising up out of the sea dwarf a human being. Yet, this imposing panorama also offers the chance of a lifetime. Adventurous souls wishing to experience the wilderness firsthand can rent remote Forest Service cabins where getting there is half the fun. Many are accessible only by boat, helicopter or floatplane. Once in the backcountry, there are opportunities for wildlife viewing, fishing, hunting or hiking. Boating enthusiasts find the Tongass a marine paradise, and canoeing and kayaking are especially popular activities in the spectacular Misty Fiords National Monument.

Above left: Mendenhall River rafting in Juneau.

Left: Sawmill at Thorne Bay.

Drying salmon reflects traditional subsistence uses of the land by native groups.

Although fishing, timber and tourism are the major industries found in the Tongass, mining is becoming increasingly significant. Rich deposits of silver, zinc and gold are excavated at Greens Creek on Admiralty Island and on Chicagof Island. Quartz Hill, near Ketchikan, has one of the largest molybdenum deposits in the world—some 1.5 billion tons of available ore. The development of mineral resources is important to the local economy as well as to the nation. Minerals are essentially buried treasure, and may someday help to balance the national trade deficit.

Treasure of a different kind is sought by archaeologists and historians in a number of sites throughout the Tongass. Fish weirs (traps), summer and winter villages, rock paintings and rock carvings are studied to learn more about the people who inhabited Southeast Alaska centuries ago. Some sites are extremely old. One, on Baranof Island, is 9,000 years old and another, on Prince of Wales Island, is 8,000 years old. Stone tools found in these locations closely resemble tools discovered in Siberia, fueling speculation that people may have entered the New World via a land bridge that once spanned the Bering Strait.

Whether it is the rich cultural heritage, the valuable resources or the pristine wilderness that one finds most compelling, all agree that the forest is truly a national treasure. And because temperate rain forests help to counter global warming, the Tongass is important to the future of the planet as well. Its beauty and significance are reminders that this magnificent place belongs to us all.

Kayaking in Tracy Arm, Tongass National Forest.

A Generous Sea

The water is alive. As the sun arcs around the sky for 19 hours a day at the peak of summer, light penetrates the nutrient-rich sea and by photosynthesis breathes life into trillions of small plants, called phytoplankton. These in turn provide nourishment for millions of small animals, called zooplankton. This living soup feeds capelin, herring and sandlance. As the food chain lengthens it includes salmon, halibut and other large fish. The eaters become the eaten and the predators the prey as the pyramid of sealife climbs to a summit of birds, porpoises, seals, otters, sea lions, whales, and people.

If we could witness a comparable eruption of life above land, it would look like an entire forest growing at a prodigious rate as far as the eye could see. Kelp can grow a foot a day. Urchins, mussels, barnacles and a dozen other invertebrates blanket the intertidal zones of Southeast Alaska shores.

The tides are extreme, rising and falling as much as 25 feet twice a day. A boat pulled up on shore during a flooding tide and left unattended for ten minutes may soon be floating away. Likewise, a rapidly ebbing tide can leave a boat high and dry on the shore until the sea returns six hours later. The range of the tides can come as a shock to campers who think, "The tide can't get this high." They awake in the middle of the night with the sea in their tents.

Extreme tides and narrow channels make for strong currents. In Wrangell Narrows, probably the most famous stretch of water in the Inside Passage, the tidal currents can exceed six miles an hour. The 70 navigational markers that twinkle red, white and green have earned Wrangell Narrows the nickname "Christmas Tree Lane." Kayakers get nowhere paddling against such odds, but when they turn around it's like running a river. The currents produce strong eddies that flush zooplankton and small fish to the surface, attracting a "feeding frenzy" of birds that dive into the water to catch a meal.

All five species of Pacific salmon migrate through the Inside Passage. Born in freshwater streams and rivers, they enter the sea to mature into adulthood before returning to spawn and die in the very spot where they were born. It's one of nature's most celebrated life cycles. Each species does things a bit differently—some lingering in freshwater, others staying out to sea—but all perform what seem to be miracles in migration and physiological ecology.

The king (or Chinook) salmon is the largest and most prized among anglers. It averages 30 pounds, but frequently tops 50 and can exceed 100 pounds. They migrate long distances through freshwater and prefer to spawn in large, mature rivers, such as the Stikine, Taku and Alsek.

Second largest is the Coho (or silver) salmon, a ready fighter that fetches high prices on the market. The sockeye (or red) salmon develops a green head and red body during spawning. Because it feeds on zooplankton and small crustaceans, it seldom bites a baited hook.

The farthest ranging salmon is the chum (or dog), so called for its rows of sharp, dog-like teeth. The smallest of the five species, averaging only 3 to 4 pounds, is the pink (or humpback) salmon, so named for the characteristic hump on the back of spawning males. The pink salmon is the most important commercially-harvested species.

Despite the salmon's reputation on the dinner plate, many folks in Southeast say the halibut, a bottomfish, makes a better meal. "Like everything else in Alaska," writes Sarah Eppenbach in *Alaska's Southeast,* "halibut come in exaggerated proportions. Halibut weighing more than 300 pounds are brought in by sport fishermen every year. The largest on record is a 495-pounder caught near Petersburg."

Other fish in Southeast are cutthroat trout, rainbow trout (also called a steelhead if it goes to sea), Dolly Varden, a member of the char family, and arctic grayling, introduced into the lakes from its native home in northern Alaska.

But when it comes to their favorite seafood dish, some residents eschew salmon and halibut and partake instead of succulent plates of king, Dungeness and tanner crab. Don't ask a group of Southeasterners which species makes the best eating, unless you've got time to listen to a colorful debate. Tens of thousands of evenings from Ketchikan to Klukwan have been spirited away in good friendship over beer, freshly-cracked crab and long-winded stories of the ones that got away.

Commercial fishing is to Southeast Alaska what farming is to Kansas. Men, women and children spend their lives on the waters of the Inside Passage. For many, home is their boat. Others fish part-time, landing deckhand positions on various types of boats that include trollers, gill-netters, purse seiners and long-liners. Old-timers say that of any twenty commercial fishermen in Southeast, the odds are that about ten will go into debt, sell their boats and get out, five will squeak by year after year, four will make a good living, and one will be a millionaire. Low fish runs, high interest rates and strict regulations can shave the profit margin down to the bare bones. Of course it's hard to assign a dollar value to the independence, the wildness, and the quiet mornings at anchor without another boat in sight.

Crab pots on the dock, Sitka Sound.

License plate and a native painting of salmon, both seen on the streets of Ketchikan.

On the Road to Recovery

There is ample reason to celebrate the existence of marine mammals in the Inside Passage, since many species here today were nearly exterminated 100 to 200 years ago. For instance, the sea otter population, once decimated along the entire southern coast of Alaska, has recently returned to the nothern waters of the Inside Passage along the shores of Chichagof and Yakobi Islands between Sitka and Icy Strait. The deep fur that keeps sea otters warm in the cool waters was known as "soft gold" by early fur seekers.

The Steller's sea lion (first identified by naturalist Georg Steller) is common along the Inside Passage. These large cousins to the California sea lion can reach sizes of up to 2,000 pounds. They are occasionally seen in Frederick Sound north of Petersburg, between Juneau and Skagway, and in Glacier Bay's rocky cliffs soaking up the sparse sunshine. All marine mammals in United States waters (except in cases of native subsistence) are protected by the Marine Mammal Protection Act of 1972.

Probably the most talked-about, watched-for, and suspense-invoking marine mammal in Southeast Alaska is *Megaptera novaeangliae,* the humpback whale. Measuring up to 45 feet long and weighing 40 tons, it sparks the excitement of cruise ship and ferry passengers when it spouts on the horizon. "There she blows," somebody shouts, breathing the atmosphere of a Herman Melville novel, and for the next half hour all eyes watch and wait. The whale might not appear again, or it might breach like a cannon shot out of the sea only a quarter mile away, crashing back into the water and leaving viewers speechless.

After giving birth to a new generation in winter waters off Hawaii and Mexico, the humpbacks return to Southeast Alaska every summer to feed on krill, herring and other small crustaceans and fish. They favor certain areas—Frederick Sound, Lynn Canal, Seymour Canal, Icy Strait and Glacier Bay—and appear to establish strict feeding territories that they defend through a behavioral repertoire of slapping their tails, rolling their 14 foot long pectoral fins and, if push comes to shove, breaching. Some scientists believe a

A congenial group of sea lions, Marble Island.

breaching whale is an aggravated whale. They contend that it may feel encroached upon by boats, ships,or other whales, and in effect may be saying, "get out."

For many years scientists studying the humpback in Southeast Alaska have been trying to determine if an increase in boating and shipping traffic correlates to a decrease in the number of whales. Do the vessels displace the whales from their feeding territories? Or do the whales stay where the food is regardless of the vessels? An estimated 15,000 humpbacks once lived in the North Pacific. Now, after a legacy of hunting and harpoons, there are fewer than 2,000. Until science can find irrefutable answers to difficult species survival questions, the humpback whale deserves the benefit of all the protection we can provide.

The minke whale, a small relative of the humpback, also summers in the Inside Passage. And like the humpback, it is a baleen whale that sifts its food through a large, kerotinous, comb-like plate, called baleen. The nomadic gray whale migrates through the Inside Passage enroute to summer feeding grounds off northern Alaska and winter breeding grounds off Mexico. Neither the minke nor the gray are sighted in Southeast Alaska nearly as often as the humpback.

That brings us to the oft-misunderstood killer whale, or Orca. This is not a whale at all, but in fact the largest member of the dolphin family. Distinguished by its large dorsal fin and distinctive black and white markings, it usually swims in groups (pods) of three to thirty animals. Like

Humpback whales feed by filtering sea water through comb-like baleen.

The magnificent flukes of a humpback.

The orca, or killer whale, has distinctive white markings.

A pod of orcas.

every other marine mammal, it is a carnivore. However, the killer whale has teeth instead of baleen, and hunts large prey such as salmon, seals and sea lions.

Often confused with the killer whale is the Dall porpoise. The markings are similar, but the Dall is only about one-third the size. It has a small dorsal fin, and often rides in the bow wake of moving boats, leaving a flashy roostertail splash. This is something a killer whale seldom does. More solitary and reserved is the harbor porpoise that feeds in the bays and coves where salmon gather to go upsteam. If we indulge in anthropomorphism for a moment, the killer whale would be the big tough guy, the Dall porpoise the fun-loving joyrider, and the harbor porpoise the quiet loner.

Last but not least is the harbor seal, the most common marine mammal in Southeast Alaska. In Glacier Bay alone an estimated 5,000 harbor seals gather on the ice floes each spring to bring forth their young. It seems a bit extreme that a newborn seal should leave a warm womb to lie on glacial ice, but the bergs offer safety from their chief nemesis, the killer whale. Birth on shore isn't a good option because of predatory wolves, wolverines and bears. It wasn't long ago when Tlingits hunted harbor seals throughout Southeast Alaska, and to this day the seals retain a distrust for humans. Yet they have a habit of raising up their heads when their curiosity is piqued. When staring back into their dark, soulful eyes we may see a vision that tells us more about ourselves than we sometimes care to know.

The Hidden Ones

Southeast Alaska has a great abundance and diversity of land animals, and an equally great ability to hide them. Living in the thick forests and nameless mountains are black bears, brown bears, Sitka black-tailed deer, moose, red squirrels, mountain goats and numerous other mammals. Seeing them from a boat is difficult, but not impossible. Observant eyes will be rewarded when a bear ambles down the shoreline or a moose swims against the tide.

Black bears feed on berries, shrubs and salmon. They often gnaw on barnacles at low tide, and seem to think nothing of swimming a mile to reach an island or opposite shore. Although most are black, they can be brown, cinnamon or even a silver-blue tone, the so-called "glacier bear."

Whereas an adult black bear averages 200 pounds, a brown bear can exceed 1,000 pounds. Admiralty, Baranof and Chichagof Islands are the main haunts for the brown bear in Southeast Alaska. Admiralty alone has about 1,700.

Sitka black-tailed deer are the most abundant large land mammal in Southeast Alaska. Small relatives of coastal mule deer, they seek high subalpine elevations in summer and descend into low elevation forests during winter. Heavy snows at times force them onto the shore to eat dried grass and seaweed. Their handsome coats range from red to gray, and are crowned with a black tail tipped with white.

When traveling the Inside Passage, watch the high rocky cliffs carefully. What appear to be spots of late summer snow may actually be mountain goats. Only a few isolated habitats support these nimble-hoofed rock climbers. Some of them are Mendenhall Glacier, Tracy Arm, Misty Fiords National Forest Monument, and Mt. Wright and Tidal Inlet in Glacier Bay.

Seeing the other land mammals of Southeast Alaska demands a walk through the forests and into the heart of more hidden country. The red squirrel is hard to miss. Often heard before it's seen, it sits on a nearby branch and berates anyone who approaches.

Its chief predator is the marten, the "North American sable." The more demure porcupine waddles away from the slightest disturbance.

Mink, beaver and other furbearers live here as well, but what breathes a truly robust quality into the land is the coyote, the wolf, and the wolverine. It takes a superb forest to support these creatures—a forest unlike most others in North America; one that few of us have a chance to see, but we can all appreciate.

Alaskan brown bears near Russell Island, Glacier Bay National Park.

Mountain goats feed on the steep mountainsides, high above a tidal inlet.

A World on the Wing

There's no shortage of birdlife in Southeast Alaska. From summits to inlets, in rain or in shine, and at all times of the year, birds make their home here. Nearly 300 species have been sighted.

But let's get right to the point. People traveling the Inside Passage for the first time usually want to see two birds above all others. One is the bald eagle, our nation's symbol, the other is the puffin, a colorful concoction that looks like something off Sesame Street, or out of a Dr. Seuss book.

You might miss the puffin, but not the bald eagle. Southeast Alaska is its stronghold. Officially listed as endangered or threatened in the lower 48 states, it thrives here where fish runs are healthy, pollution is low and respect from humans is high. But times haven't always been good for the eagle along the Inside Passage. In 1917 a bounty was imposed at $2 per bird, and by 1953 when it was lifted, 128,000 eagles had been killed under the mistaken notion that they competed with fishermen for fish. Biologists have since learned that eagles do eat healthy fish, but not in great abundance if spawned salmon are available.

Remarkably, the eagles recovered. They can be seen along the entire length of the Inside Passage. They perch in shoreline conifers, turning their regal, white heads with unblinking, predatory eyes. A white head and tail denote a sexually mature bird at least four to six years old; immature birds are completely dark.

Perhaps the greatest of all eagle spectacles happens every fall and winter on the Chilkat River, just upstream of Haines, when as many as 3,000 eagles gather to feed on a late spawning run of chum salmon.

They crowd the river banks twenty to a tree and three to a limb. In local accounts they are described as "thick as pigeons on a park bench," or "gulls at the dump." Wildlife photographers and bird watchers from around the world arrive to see this miracle of eagles.

Two species of puffins, the horned and tufted, visit Southeast Alaska each summer to nest on protected cliffs and islands. Each pair lays only one egg. Like murres, guillemots, cormorants and other seabirds that share islands with them, puffins have heavy bodies designed to dive underwater and catch fish. They might look comical to us, bouncing atop the water to take flight and flapping their wings frantically to stay aloft, but they're masterfully designed birds shaped and tested for survival at sea. Nature gives every form a function, and the puffin is no exception.

A much more angelic flier is the arctic tern, a summer visitor and a champion of avian migration that travels 22,000 miles round trip every year between Alaska and Antarctica. Other long distance fliers that nest here include several species of swallows—barn, tree and violet-green—all of them winter residents of the jungles of Central and South America.

Name any ecological niche in Southeast Alaska

Tufted puffin, Glacier Bay.

A trio of Pigeon Guillemots, Sealers Island.

Above: Bald eagle landing in the Chilkat Eagle Sanctuary, near Haines. Inset: A mature bald eagle.

and at least one species of bird, and probably more, will be there to fill it. The mating songs of the hermit thrush and varied thrush ring through the forests every summer in melodic counterpoint to the low drumming of the male blue grouse. Other forest nesting birds include kinglets, warblers, sparrows, juncos and jays, and the always raucous ravens and crows.

Snow buntings land atop glaciers and snowfields to feed on ice worms and wind-blown seeds, while not far away water pipits make a living in chaotic, boulder-strewn country deglaciated only a few years ago. And not far from the pipits live families of rock ptarmigan. On the open water might be a solitary pair of marbled murrelets, or a great raft of phalaropes or scoters that take flight in unison like a rising, winged cloud. Geese, gulls, scaups, teals, goldeneyes, mergansers, grebes and loons are out there, too.

Finding this rich variety of birdlife takes patience and open senses, the kind of traits the wilderness teaches. One could spend a lifetime looking through binoculars in Southeast Alaska, and the rewards would be well worth it. As an old Tlingit in Hoonah said, "I can't imagine this land without eagles and ravens and the others. They are the roots of our legends. They teach us to laugh and to share, and they tell us what was here before our time. What greater wisdom is there than that?"

CHAPTER THREE

AN INSIDE PASSAGE TOUR

Ketchikan

Left: Punchbowl Lake, Misty Fiords National Monument. Above: Decorated native hall at Totem Bight State Park, Ketchikan.

Ketchikan is a dirty sleeves town where men smoke like pulp mills and talk about diesel engines. They take local issues seriously and have a way of leaning into their subjects. Yet behind an untrimed beard can be an "ah shucks" grin with a missing tooth and a "glad to meet ya" sincerity. These people seem to live, more than make a living. They work hard and play hard, going to sea or to the mill or down to the local bar and restaurant with an easy going demeanor. There's no reason to move too fast in Ketchikan. It might be the fourth largest town in Alaska, but nothing worth having is ever far away.

Rusted pick-up trucks roll down the streets next to shiny new tour buses. The most popular tourist attraction in town is Creek Street—a rambling concoction of picturesque shops set on stilts and interconnected by a boardwalk. Sooner or later visitors discover Creek Street used to be Ketchikan's red light district, where, the locals say, "both fish and fishermen went upstream to spawn."

Ketchikan is a town of titles. The "Rain Capital," people call it, referring to its average of 154 inches a year. The rain can fall an inch a day for a month, and residents commonly say, "If you can't see Deer Mountain, it's raining; and if you can see it, it's about to rain." Another tall title is "Salmon Capitol of the World,"—and the records prove them right. After all, Ketchikan was born and raised on the salmon industry.

Visit nearby Totem Bight State Historical Park or The Totem Heritage Center and Ketckikan will seem like a capitol of native art as well. Dozens of Tlingit, Haida and Tsimsian totems rise in unrestored, time-honored splendor.

But of all Ketchikan's titles the one most relevant to visitors is "Alaska's First City." Thousands of first impressions are born here every year as northbound passengers disembark cruise ships and ferries to set foot in a land of their dreams, the Last Frontier. The people of Ketchikan have a talent for making those first impressions good ones.

Ancient petroglyphs on the beach, Wrangell.

Wrangell

Along the entire length of the Southeast Alaska Coast, from the bottom of the panhandle to the St. Elias Range, only a few rivers slice through the mountains from the interior to the sea. One of the largest is the mighty Stikine, 330 miles long and lined with history. Among the many peoples and places it helped to create is the town called Wrangell.

It was inevitable that competition between the British Hudson's Bay Company and the Russian-America Fur Company would come to a head in Alaska. The British controlled the interior, the Russians had the coast, and as the British inched down the Stikine River to expand their territory, the Russians reacted. They sent Captain-Lieutenant Dionysious Zarembo to cut the British off by building a sturdy fort near the mouth of the river. The Russian flag was raised over Redoubt [Fort] Saint Dionysius in August, 1834.

The British retreated. But they eventually leased the coast from the Russians (for 2,000 otter skins a year) and took command of the fort, changing its name to Fort Stikine. It became an active trading center, was later abandoned, and was jolted back to life under the American flag in the 1860s and 70s when gold seekers scrambled up the Stikine River to strikes in the Canadian Interior. By the time the gold fever ebbed, the town of Wrangell had built a sawmill and a couple canneries—not much, but it was enough of an economic base to keep the town alive.

Wrangell was on the maps to stay. Born in an act of defiance, and raised under three flags - Russian, British and American—it was a town not about to die. To this day Wrangell preserves a bit of that defiant character. It's an independent, anachronistic little town. You can walk the length of Front Street in ten minutes, but the impressions will last for ten years.

Petersburg

"Welcome to Little Norway," local residents say. "This is Scandinavia by the sea." There's no mistaking Petersburg. Hand-painted shutters frame the windows, forests of boat masts fill the harbor, halibut motifs highlight the buildings, luxurious gardens ring the homes, wooden piers reflect in the water, and every street is named for a famous fishing boat from the "old fleet." Artists return here every year to paint some of their favorite oils and watercolors. Petersburg is a place you want to take home with you.

The buildings have corroded a bit, and the pilings smell lightly of creosote and salt, but the charm, if anything, has grown stronger. Here's a town that refuses to foresake its heritage. Petersburg is the steady, stable old salt, not the boom and bust gambler chasing gold and other wildcard dreams. It lends a dime to strangers and offers a home to good friends. And it never makes a visitor feel unwelcome.

It all started in 1897 when a Norweigan named Peter Buschmann migrated to Alaska with his wife and eight children to homestead on the northern tip of Mitkof Island. Here was everything he dreamed of: a natural harbor, an abundance of halibut, salmon, crab and shrimp, an equal abundance of timber, and a constant supply of icebergs

Wharf-side Petersburg with a backdrop of snow-covered mountains. Right: The Sons of Norway shield.

(from the nearby LeConte Glacier) to pack seafood for shipment south. Other Norwegians followed Buschmann and by 1900 a proud and prosperous enclave of Scandinavia had taken root in Southeast Alaska.

The prosperity continues today. Every May Petersburg rekindles its Scandinavian spirit in the Little Norway Festival. Open to one and all, the festival is rich with polkas and waltzes in traditional dress, and homecooked meals serving everything from lutefisk to gravadlox to lefse and welskringle. People dance the days and nights away. But when the festival ends and everyone goes back to work, the spirit of new friendships and old traditions carry them through the year with the promise of an even grander festival next spring.

Sitka

Sitka is the old man by the sea. Founded by the Russians in 1804, it stands on the shore like a venerated, salt-encrusted sailor. It's the oldest white settlement in Southeast Alaska. And arguably the most beautiful, too.

It was the Russian capital in America, and the first U.S. Territorial capital in Alaska. In the early 1840s, when San Francisco consisted of just a Spanish presidio and a few wooden buildings, Sitka was the busiest harbor on the west coast of North America. On any given day, a dozen ships bound for the Orient would have been filling their holds with sea otter pelts, and the docks would have been busy with a vibrant mix of Tlingits, Russians and Aleuts.

The mix is a bit different today, but it's still vibrant. Sitka's history greets visitors at every turn. At one end of town is the Sheldon Jackson College and Museum with its rich repository of Native Alaskan artifacts. The college library reportedly has the most extensive collection statewide of literature about Alaska. James Michener, the Pulitzer prize-winning novelist, lived here for two years while he worked on his novel about Alaska.

A short walk away at the other end of town is Saint Michael's Russian Orthodox Cathedral, an architectural allegory of Sitka's past. Standing midway down Lincoln Street, it rises into twin Byzantine domes and spires that offer a pleasant contrast to the other rooftops. The original cathedral, built in the 1840s, burned to the ground in 1966. The priceless Russian icons inside would have been lost had not the people of Sitka dashed in to save them. By 1976, the cathedral had been reconstructed and the cherished icons were placed inside once again.

Attractive art shops, book stores and bakeries line Sitka's streets and easily command one's attention, but don't let them lead you astray of the stone staircase that climbs to what many believe is "the single most significant site" in Alaska's history—Castle Hill. This is where the chief managers of the Russian-American Fur Company lived after the Battle of Sitka in 1804, and where, on October 18, 1867, the Russian flag was lowered and the Stars and Stripes raised over Alaska. Silent cannons and a rock wall ring the historic hilltop today, overlooking a magnificent view of Sitka Harbor and the outlying islands.

Other points of interest include the restored Russian Bishop's House, the National Park Service visitor center, and Sitka National Historical Park. The park preserves the battlefield and Kiksadi fort site, and keeps records of the historic interactions between the Russian and native Tlingit cultures.

Left: Saint Michael's Cathedral, a Sitka landmark.
Right: Painted house posts at Sitka National Historical Park.

Log cabin and modern government building symbolize the past—and present—of Juneau, Alaska's capital.

Colorful downtown Juneau.

Juneau

Juneau is half city, half town. The capital of Alaska, its pace can be as slow as a local fisherman waiting for salmon, or as frantic as a state legislator fighting a filibuster. Out the window of a modern computer store are rows of float planes cleated to the dock and surrounded by trollers, seiners, ketches and schooners. There's a bonafide French pastry shop up the street, plus a Mexican restaurant, a foreign films theater, the Governor's Mansion, the Red Dog Saloon (complete with sawdust on the floor) and the S.O.B.—State Office Building. Everybody seems to know everybody else in Juneau. Walking downtown is a matter of going from one pleasant distraction to another, stopping every few minutes to chat with a friend or an acquaintance. It can take an hour to go three blocks.

As radically as professions stand apart in Juneau, they also dissolve together. A legislator and a commercial fisherman might meet for

The Mendenhall Glacier.

lunch, one of them sporting a suit and tie, the other wearing rubber boots and suspenders. Or they could very well be the same man, or woman, at different times of the day, or year. Yesterday a legislator, today a fisherman. And tomorrow, who knows? Don't put anything beyond a Juneauite. For the most part they are intelligent, well-educated, aggressive and young; many haven't been around just the block, they've been around the world.

Juneau boasts of having "the most accessible glacier in the North America"—the Mendenhall (you can drive right to it). But Alaskans farther north add that Juneau also has "the least accessible airport in North America." Sandwiched between steep mountains and the sea, the airport is often buffeted by winds or veiled in fog.

Several referendums have been introduced to move the state capital up to Anchorage, Fairbanks or someplace in between. Juneau has thwarted these efforts every time, most recently by a very slim margin, and Juneauites have since rebuilt their airport and spruced up their "city" to insure that their capital (and their livelihood) isn't stolen away. Of Southeast Alaska's 60,000 residents, half live in Juneau. And many of them are federal, state or city employees.

Looking east from across Gastineau Channel one sees Juneau as it should be seen—a cloister of new buildings mixed with the old, boats working the waterfront, float planes taking off and landing. All this is dwarfed by the backdrop of Mts. Juneau and Roberts rising like a wall directly behind. It seems an improbable place for a settlement, but it's where Richard Harris and Joe Juneau found gold in 1880. And nothing so engendered haphazard growth in the 19th century as the discovery of gold.

Juneau holds onto that same wild inertia today—the drive to make good wages, savor good friends and have grand adventures. There's always something going on here. There's always a way to match aspirations with accomplishments. Juneau is the boom town that never busted.

Haines

Haines is a jack of all trades. Founded in 1879 as a presbyterian mission, it soon evolved into a fishing and cannery town, and by the turn of the century was prospering in the wake of the Klondike Gold Rush. Fort William H. Seward came next. Completed in the early 1900s, it was the only active army post in Alaska for many years.

Two important transportation seeds took root in Haines in the 1940s. One was the Alaska Marine Highway System, which has since matured into an impressive fleet of ferries that run as far south as Seattle and as far north as Skagway in Southeast Alaska. The other was the Haines Highway, the only year-round overland link between Southeast Alaska and the outside world, carrying a stream of commercial and private vehicles to and from the Yukon.

In 1982 the Chilkat Bald Eagle Preserve was established just outside of town. Each fall and winter along a 20 mile stretch of the Chilkat River, paralleling the Haines Highway, 3,000 bald eagles (give or take several hundred) gather to feed on a late run of chum salmon. Truckers and locals aren't the only ones found on the highway in November these days. There are photographers from New York and London with 800mm lenses trying to get the cover shots for wildlife magazines. Senator Howard Baker has been in town with his camera, and Charles Kerault with his film crew. They come to find eagles, and Haines is happy to oblige them.

Haines is a town that dabbles in fishing, logging, transportation, tourism, and whatever else it takes to survive. It has more artists and craftspeople per capita than any other Southeast Alaska community, save maybe Gustavus. It's the Greenwich Village of the Inside Passage. And surrounding it all is scenery not even the finest paintings or prose can capture. But the artists in Haines love to try.

Above: Bald eagles fill the trees at the Chilkat Eagle Sanctuary, near Haines.

Left: A rustic cabin along the Chilkat River.

Skagway

Skagway is a poke of gold, a ragtime song, a slanted boardwalk, a horse and buggy, a streetside melodrama, a graveyard party, a roving musician, a softball game, and a candlelight parade. And that's just the beginning. The rest you have to see to believe.

When 200,000 cruise ship and ferry passengers arrive to stroll the streets each summer, Skagway explodes into a carnival atmosphere. It isn't as crazy as those gold-hungry days in 1898 when lawless men ate cigars, drank bad whiskey and shot and killed each other, but it's crazy nonetheless. It's a fun, exuberant place. One doesn't witness history in Skagway, one lives it. From the end of the dock to the middle of town is a 10 minute walk into the Roaring 1890s.

Skagway is at the end of the line of the Inside Passage, 1,141 miles north of Seattle. Miners called it "Gateway to the Klondike." They disembarked from steamers here and by the tens of thousands began their long, overland treks into the goldfields of Canada's Yukon Territory.

The town grew like fireweed and lupine in a valley beneath snow- capped peaks. It was a town of great ambitions and of tricky pitfalls. Jefferson Randolph "Soapy" Smith, preeminent Skagway badman, had a loose crew of 200 conmen and bunco artists who worked the streets inventing countless ways to pilfer the pockets of innocent stampeders. Some miners had the packs stolen off their backs before they even hit the trail. Frank Reid finally killed Soapy in a gunfight, but not before Soapy fired a round into Reid that ended his life 12 painful days later. Both are buried in Skagway's Gold Rush Cemetery, yet the town refuses to let them die, especially Smith. His name lives on in parlors, books and in the most beloved melodramas. Leave it to Skagway to immortalize the bad over the good; it's a trait of any rambunctious town.

In September, when the last cruise ship leaves, things close down, including the Klondike Highway. Many merchants migrate South. Others settle in for the long winter hibernation to carve wooden spoons or to knit wool sweaters.

Such is Skagway, an island of human character in a sea of wilderness. It makes the most of its time and place, lying dormant in the winter and erupting with life in the summer, just like the fireweed and the lupine.

A modern "Soapy Smith" in the Red Onion Saloon, Skagway.

Curio shops line Skagway's Broadway.

Glacier Bay National Park & Preserve

On a cold, rainy day in October, 1879, a canoe with six men entered a nameless bay somewhere in the uncharted waters of Southeast Alaska. Fog veiled the surrounding land, and as the canoe moved up the bay, icebergs began to tower ahead. Four Tlingits paddled nervously as a presbyterian minister intoned words of deliverance. In the bow, with his face into the wind and his wild blue eyes the color of glacial ice, an exuberant naturalist urged them onward.

Eventually the icebergs grew too thick for the party to continue, and they went ashore. The naturalist scaled a mountainside to behold a view preserved in his words to this day: "Climbing higher for still a broader outlook, I made precious time while sunshine streamed through the luminous fringes of the clouds, and fell on the glittering bergs, the crystal bluffs of the two vast glaciers, and the intensely white, far spreading fields of ice, and the ineffably chaste and spiritual heights of the Fairweather Range, which were now hidden, now partly revealed, the whole making a picture of icy wildness unspeakably pure and sublime."

Exploring an ice cave inside the Muir Glacier. Right: Icebergs reflected in the calm waters of Muir Inlet.

John Muir had found Glacier Bay. He returned three times over the next 20 years and each time the glaciers had retreated farther up the bay, sometimes as rapidly as a mile a year. His descriptions in popular magazines and scientific journals sparked readership across the continent. Here was a land of massive geological and ecological processes, but all accelerated into a human timeclock. Things were happening in years, not in thousands of years. It was a place with a pulse; a place where change itself was the only constant.

It's no different today. Drama unfolds every year as the great ice rivers move. In the last 200 years a single massive glacier that completely filled Glacier Bay has retreated 65 miles and branched into a dozen smaller tributary glaciers now sequestered at the ends of their inlets. Some continue to retreat, some have stabilized, and a few have begun to advance.

A new land has emerged from beneath the ice, and with it a living chronology of vegetation. Plant communities arrive one after another, establish themselves, and are succeeded by a new community. It begins with the pioneering dwarf fireweed and mountain avens, followed by the seral alder and cottonwood, and finally, a century after the glacier departs, a climax forest of spruce and hemlock takes root. The land is healing. The evolving patterns of vegetation create new habitats that in turn attract wildlife. Moose, bears, mountain goats, wolves and squirrels have arrived, as have fish, seals, porpoises and whales. Add to them a rich compliment of birds. All this life is found in an environment completely buried by ice 200 years ago.

Glacier Bay is not a collection of individual components, but rather a living laboratory of interrelationships. It's a land of processes. Put them all together and it becomes an abridged chapter of the evolutionary history of the earth. Traveling up the bay from its forested southern end to the icy northern end is more than a journey through geography—it's a journey through time. You begin in the present and finish in the past, staring face to face into the crystalline blue walls of the Ice Age.

Left: The little community of Elfin Cove. Above: A magnificent brown bear, Admiralty Island. Right: Water cascades into Walker Cove, Misty Fiords National Monument. Far Right: Kayaking in Misty Fiords.

The ABC Islands —Admiralty, Baranof & Chichagof

Nobody typifies life on Admiralty Island like the old homesteader, Stan Price. "Well," he says, "I got a lot of bears around my place. I like it that way. They were here first and they put up with me. I'd rather have them around here than a bunch of dogs."

The Tlingits call Admiralty Island *Kootznahoo,* or "Bear Fortress." These aren't black bears, but Alaska brown bears. Wildlife biologists estimate Admiralty has an average of approximately one brown bear for each of its 1,700 square miles. And with one or more bald eagle nesting trees for each of its 678 miles of shoreline, Admiralty Island can boast the greatest concentration of nesting bald eagles in the world. Recognized for its tremendous wilderness, wildlife and cultural values, Admiralty Island became a National Forest Monument in 1980. Its resources are administered by the Forest Serivce. The only permanent settlement on Admiralty is Angoon, a small town founded on whaling that has since turned to fishing.

Baranof and Chichagof Islands have several communities ringing their shores. Hoonah, on the north shore of Chichagof, is the largest Tlingit settlement in Alaska. Legends say that when the great ice came down from the mountains and buried their village in Glacier Bay, probably 5,000 to 7,000 years ago, the Tlingits paddled south to safety and founded their new home, Hoonah. Equally charming are the hamlets of Pelican, Elfin Cove, and the ever popular Tenakee Springs, where hot sulfur water pours over the shoulders of smiling bathers the a rate of 7 gallons a minute. Tenakee Springs has plenty of paths, but no roads. The residents like it that way.

In these remote communities is the essence of smalltown Southeast Alaska. The buildings, the walkways, the piers—even life itself—seem to linger in benign neglect. It's the kind of place that brings out the Huckleberry Finn in people.

Misty Fiords National Monument

Take California's Yosemite Valley with its tall granite walls and ribbon-like waterfalls. Add interludes of more gentle topography covered with thick blankets of hemlock, spruce and cedar. Dissect it with long, narrow fjords that reach deep into the land. Finally, cover it with a leaden sky and let the rain fall two out of every three days. What have you got? Misty Fiords National Monument, 2.2 million acres of wilderness.

Float planes and tour boats depart Ketchikan daily in the summer to visit Misty Fiords. It's not on the main route to anywhere, but it's well worth the side trip. Kayakers have a habit of paddling through these fjords and returning home with a contented look that comes only from a solid week in the wild. Fishermen say Misty Fiords is home to some of Alaska's richest salmon spawning grounds. When U.S. Borax arrived and sought to mine for molybdenum—a potential threat to the fish habitat and to the wilderness integrity—it was kayakers and fishermen who journeyed side by side to Washington D.C. in the late 1970s to fight for the creation of Misty Fiords National Monument. As a result, tight environmental protection standards now aim to keep this country as it has always been—wild, clean, and therapeutic to the human body, mind and soul.

THE BACK OF BEYOND

This book barely scratches the surface. There's so much more out there. Tracy Arm, for example, is not far from Juneau and is considered by many to be the single most spectacular piece of scenery in the Inside Passage. But others take issue, siding with LeConte Bay, near Petersburg, or with Ford's Terror, or with any of a dozen other places. And don't forget the small settlements that punctuate the scenery now and then with endemic flavor, from the once mighty Chilkat Tlingit stronghold of Klukwan up north, to the Tsimshian Indian colony of Metlakatla down south. These places are on the paths less traveled by, lying in the fringes and hollows of the back of beyond. There are dozens of them, all within reach, and each and every one is worth a visit.